please look into the mirror

michaela angemeer

Please Look into the Mirror copyright © 2024 by Michaela Angemeer. No part of this book may be used or reproduced in any manner whatsoever without written permission except in the case of reprints in the context of reviews.

michaelapoetry.com | @michaelapoetry

Cover art by McKenzie Parrott | @parrottpaints

Interior artwork by Michaela Angemeer

ISBN: 978-1-7752727-6-2

praise for please look into the mirror

Michaela's voice of vulnerability and honesty provides readers a space to reflect upon their emotions and experiences. *Please Look into the Mirror* is a testament to the power of language to impact and heal the heart.
— Whitney Hanson, author of *Harmony*

An unfiltered and unapologetic call to be present and heal the mother wound. *Please Look into the Mirror* arrives at the perfect time. In a world filled with chaos, we need to look inward more than ever, and Angemeer's raw vulnerability invites us to do just that.
— Christopher Tapp, author of *may i come home*

Please Look into the Mirror is for those searching for the validation they never received in their childhood, those repairing familial relationships, and those learning to accept themselves. Angemeer's words reminded me why I stay alive for little me; for that, I am so grateful.
– ari b. cofer, author of *unfold: poetry + prose*

A story of reconnecting with the self at every age, through every step of emotional growing pains—told through Angemeer's classically profound yet graspable voice. A must-read for softening into one's own identity.
— Kim Rashidi, author of *Girl Mess*

Michaela beautifully guides you to take your inner child by the hand and break your own generational trauma by giving them the love and healing they—and you—so desperately need.

— Parker Lee, author of *coffee days whiskey nights*

for mom,
my first mirror

i just wanna be a reflection
of all the love i've ever received

contents

glass..11
mirror..39
reflection..83

"It is astonishing the lengths to which a person, or a people, will go in order to avoid a truthful mirror."

–James Baldwin

glass

[/glas/]
noun

> 1. a hard, brittle substance, typically transparent or translucent, made by fusing sand with soda, lime, and sometimes other ingredients and cooling rapidly

> 2. an optical instrument or device that has one or more lenses and is designed to aid in the viewing of objects not readily seen

i wish i could play in the sand again
before i knew to worry about it
getting stuck in my bottoms

i know time is cyclical
because at thirty-one

i'm twelve again
longing for mom to blow dry my hair
begging my brother
to watch movies in the basement

i'm nine again
crying when
my friends move away
reading books under the covers

i'm four again
responding with a roar
when my dad asks if i'm a bear
breathing in deep at the hardware store

i'm one again
i don't know what this world wants from me
i just know i'm tired
i just know i need rest

brushing my hair for little me
eating breakfast for little me
playing in the lake for little me
planting flowers for little me
laughing loud for little me
saying no for little me
crying for little me
staying alive for little me

"what does your inner child need?"

a hug / to jump in a puddle / gummy bears / an ice cream sundae / reassurance / a box of sixty-four crayons / finger paints / a lullaby / to be kissed by the ocean / to play with a puppy / a sleepover / to laugh with friends / to build a sand castle / stability / a bubble bath / to make friendship bracelets / a cold glass of lemonade / sidewalk chalk / affection / a water balloon fight / to roll down a hill / to make art without worrying if it's good

I AM NOT A DISAPPOINTMENT

how many times
will i scream mother
at someone who didn't birth me
before i realize
i don't get a do-over

your children don't want to be
the only thing you're proud of

please look into the mirror

my mother was
a shrinking woman
how could she fit all of us
put us first
without getting smaller

my mother was so fragile
she gave me a glass pedestal
i lifted her onto it diligently
knelt beside it
dug my shins into the ground
maybe if i buried my body
permanently beneath her
i would be worthy of her love
maybe if she didn't have to
see herself in me
she could be happy

please look into the mirror

our mothers treat our bodies
as if they are weapons
because it's easier to tell us
to conceal them
than disarm the bombs
within our brothers

emergency contact

don't call mom or dad
call my brother
he might not pick up
right away
but he will eventually
he might not hold your feelings
but at least he has some sanity

if you knew it would still affect me
eighteen years later
would you have done it

i always thought my mom would love me more
if i was prettier
i'd spend hours painting myself in the mirror
so i'd be less of a mirror for her
maybe she would love me more
if i looked less like her

not enough / too much

i wish i felt loved by the way my parents loved me
but i didn't

so now i look for love in the trees and flowers
maybe i'll find it in the ocean
i know it's in your eyes
i can always see it when i look in your eyes

but seeing is different than feeling
and lately all i've been feeling is numb
i know i've known love

my chest has swelled so much my heart almost burst
but right now i need a magnifying glass
i can't see it
i can't feel it

i need to be quiet so i can hear it
but my mind always has other plans

i wish i could feel all the love
that has ever been felt for me all at once
without worrying about whether i'll be able to handle it
whether it's too much for me
whether i'm too much for me?

but maybe instead
i'll just write another poem
about how when i look in the mirror
my mother looks right back
and though i don't know for sure
i think she wishes
that when she was a little girl
she felt loved by the way her parents loved her too

IT HURTS
and
I'M ALLOWED
TO SAY
SOMETHING
ABOUT IT

i've been homesick my whole life
missing a home i never had

please look into the mirror

all it takes is one photo
that i didn't take
to send me back into a spiral
of do i really look like that
and are those my proportions
is that a double chin
all it takes is one
to create a thousand
bad thoughts about myself
i can't find the exit
by reminding myself i'm prettier in person
or that the camera adds ten pounds
ten pounds mean nothing
when you'd rather not exist
and when i can't spin anymore
when i've spent all the hate
the world gave me to give
all that's left to remember is that
though my mother was my first bully
i was my second

if mom didn't sell
my childhood home
i would go back and
smash the full-length hallway mirror
hours spent
posing
contorting
shrinking
fixating
criticizing
sit in front of the mirror so you eat less
hoping for my body to change
and it did
but i couldn't see it
because i altered
the neural pathways in my brain

i do so much thinking
i could gaslight myself into anything

permission to speak, sir?
permission to be loud
actually
permission to be even louder
permission to not brush my teeth today
permission to keep my hair in the same bun for a week
permission to not know
permission to be silly
permission to be funny
permission to be beautiful
actually
permission to not care about beauty for one day
permission to just be me
permission to be ugly

remember life before you knew about gas prices
before you knew who was president
or what left and right meant
in a political sense

remember life before you knew about paying rent
utilities or a mortgage
when your biggest challenge
was learning to tie your shoes

remember life before you understood money
before you heard the word capitalism
before you saw your parents suffer because of it
before you could name it

remember life before you knew about death
when you thought we'd just play pretend for all eternity
no worry about the afterlife
or guilt or shame or the original sin

remember life?
remember living?
remember what it was like to breathe easy?
do remember yourself?

what if i am not my mother
or my father
but something else

what if i am their alchemy
what they didn't get the chance to be
what if i am a third more hopeful thing

the record keeper

when you grow up as the only one in your family who notices the dysfunction, you feel overly compelled to remember it. you take note of every slight. of every yell. of every eggshell you walk on. of the tears that were shed, sometimes out of sight. it was at least sixteen tears today. or wait, did that first one count? was it actually seventeen?

you keep these notes, you record everything diligently, you categorize and file. by the time you leave home you have a rolltop desk that will barely close. but you can't get rid of anything. because if you don't keep these records, no one else will.

as you get older and try to reconcile who you were with who you are now, you can't help but keep bringing up the records. but every time you pull out a file, date and time stamped, you're met with blank stares.

"i don't remember it like that."
"are you sure that's how it happened?"
"well, it was only one time."

and you scream and you cry and you plead for someone else to remember it like you did. how could they not remember the events that shaped you? why can't they see their wrongdoings? how will you ever get an apology, how will you ever know peace if no one else cares about the records?

but then you get even older. and you start to realize that though these records helped you as a child. though they were the only proof, the only validation that things went wrong, there are some you can let go of now. you no longer need the exact details. you no longer need to convince everyone that everything did happen as you remember. because the truth is, you can't force people to see themselves in a way they're not ready to acknowledge.

slowly you'll realize that your acknowledgment of these events is enough. and they happened. and you'll wrestle the rolltop open. and you'll start to rip up the files.

"your memories are valid."
"you are seen."
"you deserved better."

and with each tear, you'll make room for new memories. because you're not a kid anymore. and you trust yourself. and the records did their job. and you can keep yourself safe now.

you can't force people to see themselves in a way they're not ready to acknowledge

mirror

[/'mirer/]
noun

1. a reflective surface, now typically of glass coated with a metal amalgam, that reflects a clear image

2. something that gives a true representation

what is my past self
if not a mirror for my current self

please look into the mirror

when did you pick all this up?
who added to it along the way?
and how long did you think
you could carry it by yourself?

even your worst year had smiles. even your worst year had sunny days. it had new episodes of a tv show you love. it had a new song you learned the words to. it had dogs to say hello to. even your worst year had new ideas. new art. new poems. new books. even your worst year had slices of cake. rogue balloons outside of a stranger's house. it had fresh air and beautiful thunderstorms. babies laughing. old people holding hands walking down the street. even your worst year had your favorite drink. a sweater in your favorite color. even your worst year had you. and i hope next year gets to know you too.

backside liturgies
(originally appeared in *the weaver: accidental altars*)

i count the spots on my back
through teary eyes
try to see Orion's Belt
or the Big Dipper
what if Cassiopeia herself
planted these blemishes
—a lesson in vanity

what if she's taking
her punishment out on me
or what if thirty-one spots
on my back
mean that thirty-one years
are behind me
Libra teaching to let go of
what's weighing me down
so that i can move forward in harmony

there hasn't been a clear sky in weeks
maybe these spots are the stars' way
of missing me
maybe they showed up
because even when i can't see it
the universe has my back
the universe is within me

i can't convince you
that you deserve to be loved by me

for the anxious

you are worthy of a love that doesn't give you heart palpitations. you are worthy of a love that's easeful, that makes you sleepy, that gives you space to rest. the right person won't make you feel like you have to catch your breath. the right person won't pull away when you push. they'll hold your hand and let you know they're right there. i know you've spent your whole life trying to convince people you're worth loving. this is your permission to stop. to pause. to rest. to receive. you just need to open your palms. the right love is right there. and it's not going anywhere.

for the avoidant

what if you didn't run, just this once? what if you took a deep breath and asked yourself what it means to trust? what if trust means staying? you are worthy of giving yourself a chance at love. maybe there's not something wrong with everyone you've ever tried to love. maybe finding their flaws is your way of protecting yourself. i know you've spent your whole life thinking that it's easier to be alone. that growing up, it was easier to be alone. it's not your fault you were taught that vulnerability equals pain. this is your permission to honor your desire for connection. to give yourself grace for your hyperindependence. to start looking at everything you love about love instead of everything that scares you.

maybe my attraction to you
was misattribution of arousal
i drank so much coffee back then
could barely decipher the thoughts in my head
and i definitely didn't know what love was
anxiety was what i was in

if i saw you again i know
i would get a grapefruit-sized pit in my stomach
and that used to make me feel shame
but now i'm just grateful to feel things so deeply
to be this alive

please look into the mirror

thought i was done with this
thought i learned a lesson or two
why do i keep giving
all my sparkle to you
can't help but look down at my shoes
how did this pedestal get back here
i thought i smashed it
it's not your fault i learned
i'm not an equal
it's not my fault i learned
to bury my needs
can it be different this time
please, can it be different
all i want is room for both of us to shine

michaela angemeer

if i leave you
who will i ask to fold the towels

please look into the mirror

maybe you want to run
because you never learned how to love
two people at the same time

two of swords

i wish i could divide
live two lives
surely one of me
would make the right decisions
choose the hard choices
learn the lessons
stop the cycles
surely one of me
would figure out all this unknown
i need more chances
more opportunities
to do this life right

i wasted so much time on guilt
counting my blessings
never forgetting my sins
praying for forgiveness
getting nothing in return
i did everything right
so why didn't it work

what is god if he could not love me
what is he
if he would damn me to hell
for all eternity
just for loving somebody
what is your god
but a judgment permit
a soulless entity that lets you
cast stones at me
is this god
is this creator? universal oneness?
or is this hate so ugly you couldn't claim it
hate so dark that god was the only thing
you could think to name it
is your god really a god at all?
or is it your own poison?
your self-hate?
my god is love, limitless
my god doesn't respond to your name

i see Gaza everywhere

when i see a thirty-year-old man in business casual attire on the street i think of my brother, and how i wish he lived closer to me. and when i see a sixty-something woman with a bob, barely five feet tall, i think of my mother, and a part of me softens. when i see a twenty-something girl with dark hair in a messy bun i think of how she could be my cousin. or twenty-five-year-old Bisan. and i hope they both survive another day, but i know the only difference between them is where on this earth their soul happened to enter their body. when i see photos of seven-year-old Sidra with her thick bangs and tie-dye sweater i can't help but think of seven-year-old me. and how Sidra deserved safety and love just like i did. and how the only reason she was a victim of a massacre and i got to become thirty-one is because of where i was born. when i see photos of six-year-old Hind i think of every little girl i've smiled at in my life. and the six-year-old i was once. and the six-year-old i hope to have some day. and how the only difference between them having a chance at life and Hind's being taken from her by a genocide is where they happened to be born. when i see someone on the street i see my face and my family's faces and every Palestinian that is miraculously still alive and the tens of thousands who aren't. i see Gaza everywhere and i wish there was more i could do than just witness it.

just because you used to like something
doesn't mean you have to anymore

just because you used to believe something
doesn't mean you have to anymore

you can learn new information
you can have new experiences
you can change your mind

this is your permission to become
to release yourself from the shackles of an identity
you no longer resonate with

when you go so long
without knowing who you are
so much is blurred
the mirror is foggy

but you wipe
and you wipe
and you wipe
and when the fog lifts

you finally see yourself
and there are two moments
joy for the brightness
for the knowing
for the self-acceptance

and grief for the past
for the time missed
for the time you'll never get back

and now although
i don't want to waste any more time
i'm learning not to rush
i get to learn this new me
at my own pace
i have this time, now
and i deserve to move slowly

mirror mirror
on the wall
who's the saddest of them all?

what's that i see?
you can't mean me
i've journaled
and gone to therapy

please look into the mirror

are you getting tired of loving me
i know sometimes it's hard to do consistently
i can be a little snarky
occasionally gloomy
at times i lack affection
it's not about you
it's usually about
how i feel about me
i hope you don't take it personally

michaela angemeer

who are you
if not a mirror for me

i'm so sad
is it the PMDD
why does being honest with you
make me think you'll leave me
i'm crying again
don't know what to say again
emailing therapists
making playlists
i don't want to come to the conclusion
that it's easier to be alone
is it my PMDD
or is it easier to be alone
or is nothing easy anymore

i'm so lonely
traffic is comforting

winter can't hold my hand
so it leads me to self-preservation
i know there is enough here
but i'm eating stale crackers
from the back of my cupboard

when the cornfields
are plowed down
and covered in snow
i wonder if they'll ever grow again
after being so cold

when i can't pick an apple
from a tree
i fear it will forget
how to bud in spring

i lost god ten years ago
and since then it's been so hard
to have faith in something
i cannot see

do i want a girlfriend
or a mother
you can't fill the gaps she left

please look into the mirror

i'm sorry you thought healing meant erasing parts of yourself. i'm sorry you thought going to therapy meant that now you could only ever say the right things. i'm sorry you were taught that being honest is mean. i'm sorry you learned to sacrifice your truth to protect other people. i'm sorry you learned you were responsible for other people's feelings. i'm sorry you thought you always had to be the bigger person. but you don't have to be. healing is not synonymous with getting rid of everything that makes you, you. you don't have to be the only person who has it all together. who thinks before you speak. sometimes your thoughts are meant to be heard, pure. sometimes you're the only one who can deliver the truth. and you're hiding your light, you're doing yourself a disservice by trying to be perfect. healing doesn't mean becoming perfect. the whole point of healing is recognizing that there was never anything wrong with you to begin with.

tried so hard to be a nice girl
that i ended up being nice to everyone
but myself

thought i learned this already
but apparently it bears repeating
saying what you feel isn't rude

sacrificing your feelings for others
is a form of self-harm
i'm unlocking the box

breaking the curse
i'm screaming again
hear me roar

i've found my voice
i have it back
and i'm never giving it up again

I WANT TO

TELL THE

TRUTH AGAIN

i'm trying to throw out
my learned behaviors
can you help me?
they're old and heavy

no more mr. nice guy
i'm mean now
i didn't notice you turning my shards
into soft sea glass
i guess that's what thirty years of
getting tossed around by waves does

no more mr. nice guy
no more always trying to say the right thing
maybe gut is more important than correct
maybe i should let it spill

no more mr. nice guy
i'm allowed to say how i feel
sacrificing my truth
to make someone comfortable
is just self-abandonment with a bow on it

no more mr. nice guy
he wasn't even real
cause the nicest thing i could do for myself
is say how i really feel

your needs are valid. you deserve to share them. you deserve to be heard. you are not responsible for people's reactions to your needs. if they can't meet them, it's up to them to say so. by suppressing your needs and not giving people the opportunity to meet them, you're suppressing yourself. you're inadvertently telling yourself that their comfort is more important than your expression. you are not a burden for needing things. and you deserve to have your needs met.

gonna become a therapist
because i miss gossip
who invented the phrase *trauma dump*
i'd like to have a word with them
why do my friends feel like they need to be
perfect for me
i want the messy
phone me on your worst day
i didn't learn to deal with all this
to do it alone
won't someone rely on me?
i love you at your best
and your worst doesn't feel like that to me
i'm your friend because you're human
i'm your friend because you're a multifaceted being

you are breaking generational patterns
by asking for help
by being honest when you're sad
by acknowledging your needs

please look into the mirror

i don't want the lines between
you and i to blur
i want us to be separate entities
i want us to keep the magic
that brought us together
my tendency to melt into you
i know it's not good for me
i need to be able to be alone
i need to have my own identity

i don't want to be alone
permanently
but i don't want to forget myself

i can only dance
like no one's watching
if no one's watching

i can only make myself laugh
and know it's not a show
if i'm the only one there

sometimes my ideas
need solitude
sometimes my heart
needs to beat just for me

i need to be alone
occasionally
to remember to love me intentionally

please look into the mirror

i apologized to three people today
turns out i was a bit of a menace
for most of my twenties
and most of the time
the bad i saw in others
was just a mirror

if i can't see myself as the villain
how will i ever grow

if my mother sees me
as all the parts of herself
she's afraid of

maybe i see her
as all the parts of myself
i'm afraid of, too

i'm tired of being
the only one who sees
my darkness is what
makes me, me
it's not scary
it's not shameful
we all have jagged edges
experiences that are painful
the more you ignore it
the more it perseveres
one finger pointed forward
the other four don't just disappear
there's nowhere to hide
i burned away the veneer
so would you please just once
look into the fucking mirror

"how are you?"

i've been practicing unclenching my jaw / counting the cracks in the sidewalk / finding shapes in the clouds / playing pretend / eating cheese and crackers / filing my nails when they chip / forgetting to shave my legs / watching my dog grow older / swallowing the lump in my throat / writing to-do lists / listening to ABBA / dipping my toes in the lake / driving past my old apartment / swallowing the lump in my throat / talking to my mom again / swallowing the lump in my throat / watching my dad grow older / swallowing the lump in my throat / watching myself grow older / i can't swallow all these lumps

my mother's mirror

last year, i saw my mom for the first time in three years.

time is a funny thing. it can do almost anything–grow, warp, distort, watch things pass by. but the only thing time can't do is preserve.

i don't think i grew any taller but my mom plus three years is a little smaller. a little sadder. she looked a little more fragile than what i remembered. than the bully that my inner child knew. than the unfaceable monster of my early adulthood. my perception changed. because those three years made me feel stronger. more resilient. less susceptible to crack at any moment.

but when i saw her sadness, i couldn't help but feel it in me. maybe this was the first time in my life where my mother's feelings weren't a projection of something else. her sadness was directly caused by the distance between us. in a way it was one of the first experiences we shared equally since my birth.

and in that moment, after those three years, i watched my mother see her reflection in me. and i watched her see me not as something that reflected all the dark parts of her. the things she wanted to forget. but i watched her see me as grief that could let go. as love, that for three whole years, had nowhere to go.

i had to be broken glass before i could stand in the mirror. really look at myself, instead of just holding up a mirror for her. instead of just being her reflection.

now, i can look right back at her. we stand facing each other. holding time in one hand and hope in the other. i don't need to be her reflection anymore. for us, time was the only thing that could separate our identities. it gave me my own mirror. and now we both get the chance to be whole.

reflection

[/rəˈflekSH(ə)n/]
noun

1. the throwing back by a body or surface of light, heat, or sound without absorbing it

2. serious thought or consideration

summer rituals

i say good morning to the neighborhood cats / smile at flowers / and the bees rolling around in their pollen / the sun makes me squint / heats my cheeks / a chipmunk runs across the street / a very large peanut in his mouth / and all at once i recognize the mirror / for i am the neighborhood cats / i am the flowers / insect wings grow from my spine / antennae seeking pollen / i am the chipmunk / i am even the peanut / and though i have this beautiful mirror in front of me / i can't stop thinking about what i want to be when i grow up / but maybe i'm not supposed to know / maybe who i am right now is more important / maybe right now i can just be the sun

before i met you
i thought i was writing love poems
but i wasn't
they were wishes
stacked on the cracked foundation
of unrequited love
they were dreams
of moss filled meadows
before i'd felt someone this soft
they were hopes
i was too scared to let come true
but you aren't a fantasy
you're as real as the earth beneath me
as steady as a river that's never suffered drought
as reliable as the sunset or Orion's belt
and the only thing i wish for now
is more days with you
i hope there are more than i can count

when i look at you
i see every person you've ever been
and i love all of them

i don't wanna grow old with someone. i wanna finger paint with someone when we're forty. play with each other's hair when we're fifty. make smiley face pancakes when we're sixty. sock puppets when we're sixty-seven. spin in the rain when we're seventy. jump in puddles when we're seventy-two. make pillow forts when we're eighty. play make-believe when we're ninety. i wanna grow young with someone. i wanna grow young with you.

what if there's no first to leave
what if you both choose to stay

sometimes it's easier
to be angry about something
than sad about it

sometimes it's easier to say
'i hate you' than
'you hurt me'

anger can take us
outside of ourselves
focusing on someone else
while sadness requires
acknowledgement of hurt within

it's ok if you'd rather yell
than cry right now
but eventually
make room for the sadness, too

what i wouldn't give to meet my mother
the same age as i am now
did she have dreams
could she name them?
did she have hopes?
did she give them all to me?

please look into the mirror

instead of trying to see myself as different from those i'm critical of, i'm starting to ask what about them triggers me? how are they showing me my own shadows? when judgment shows up is it because i'm really that different? or are we mostly the same?

don't you see you were always wanted?

i wish you flexibility. a life with more understanding. i know trauma has made it easier to think in black and white. to cut people off. to not give second chances. but as you learn to be more gentle with yourself, are there ways you can extend that to others too? to realize that some things are forgivable. and just like you are imperfect, so are the people you love. what if you acknowledged that hurting each other is a part of the human experience? what if you realized that hurt is an opportunity to learn how to repair instead of further isolating yourself?

i thought it was normal
or at least common
to always feel like something was wrong
to wait with baited breath
not a question of if the other shoe will drop
i can already hear it falling
heart rate one hundred
or close
i'm too afraid to check it
but my doctor gave me a checklist
turns out this apple
is still hanging from her father's tree
so i'm trying medication
i'm getting help
for my brain that's a little different
it has adhd

you're not in trouble. no one's mad at you. you didn't do anything wrong. you're human. take a deep breath and let that sinking feeling go. you have a good heart. you care about people. no one expects you to do everything perfectly. part of what makes you special is your mistakes, your flaws. you're learning and growing, just like everyone else. you're trying your best, and that's all you can ask of yourself. give yourself a little forgiveness, a little grace. you're here. you showed up. you deserve to be proud of yourself.

I DON'T WANT TO BE MOTIVATED BY SHAME AND FEAR

this is your permission to do things half way. to use mouthwash instead of brushing your teeth. to take out half the garbage. to wash your body but not your hair. to have cereal for lunch and dinner. to only throw your underwear into the wash. to put on a clean shirt but keep your pajama pants on. if you're not feeling one hundred percent, it can feel impossible to do anything. so why not do small things that make you feel better? your twenty-five percent, your fifty percent, your sixty-seven percent is good enough too. and they can slowly help you get back to one hundred.

what if self-compassion let you see that you deserve to take care of yourself? because you love yourself, not because you're lacking? what if you didn't have to judge or hate your way into changing your behavior? what if you could love yourself into the life you want?

today, let yourself feel joy.
for the fact that you're still here.
for the fact that in spite of it all, you're still trying.

when the blue jay visits
i know i'll be okay
a sign from my ancestors
that my blood will keep flowing today
that i'll notice the trees
and their new growth
that i'll take more deep breaths
a blue jay is their oath
and though it might feel dark right now
this bird is here today
to remind me of my strength
and protectors
that my dreams are on their way

for the impatient

it's tempting to want everything to unfold straight away. to figure out all the mysteries. to dispel the unknown. to receive all your blessings at once. but there is so much beauty in the unfolding. the natural timing of things. maybe something you thought you so badly needed in your twenties will unfold so much more graciously in your thirties. maybe something you thought you'd accomplish in your thirties will unravel so much more deliciously in your forties. there is no need to rush. everything is happening at the exact perfect pace. slow down and enjoy the unfolding.

having patience with others is the same thing as having patience with yourself. when you force yourself to do something quickly, you're ignoring your natural flow. by rushing, you miss out on the magic that time wants to gift you. when you rush others, you dishonor the flow of your reciprocation. you deny them their own magic, their own need for alchemy. when you accept your own timing and the timing of others, you learn how to trust, building a universe where time is abundant.

what if everything is happening exactly how it's supposed to?

i'm never sucking in my stomach again
i wish i could time travel
to before i knew to shame it
would it be three
maybe two
before i knew most things
i knew i needed to hold it in
what if this belly is joy
it deserves jiggle
what if i'm not holding in my stomach
i'm holding in my self-hate
giving it a home
in this breathless chest
i'm never sucking in my stomach again
i choose air
i choose me

for the overthinkers

you are right here, right now in this moment. you are alive. you are safe. your feet are planted on the ground. you can breathe. take a deep breath. three in. three out. so much happened yesterday, and the day before, and the day before that. and so much will happen tomorrow. next month. this year. but right now you can be still. you can sink into this very moment. you don't need to worry about what you have or don't have. what you want. what you're scared of. what if this moment has everything you need? what if all it takes is taking the time to notice it?

i emptied my cup
sat there alone
for what felt like centuries
waited for peace
waited for a sign
and slowly stardust
started falling
now i can choose
what i accept as love
who deserves to live in my cup
on terms that honor me
and my journey

new moon prayer

i put down fear
and welcome the unknown
i hold gratitude for everything i love
and all that i have
i open doors for blessings that are
unfathomable right now
i put my faith in the universe
i put my faith in me

full moon prayer

i thank my life for all that it's given me
i hold on to the lessons of the past,
whisper to them softly
i let go of the rest,
let it be turned into something new
a lesson for someone else

please look into the mirror

what do plants teach us
if not to remove
the dead weight
to make room for new growth

i'm proud of you for waking up today. i'm proud of you for being here. i'm proud of you for sticking with it even when it's dark and cold. i'm proud of you for all your yesterdays, your today and your tomorrows. i'm proud of you for taking another chance on yourself, even if it's hard. even if you really didn't want to. i'm proud of you for showing up to another day and saying i'm here. i'm me. it's all i have right now, and it's enough to be proud of.

it's okay to be scared. it's okay to lose your breath. to close your eyes and leap. to not know where you'll land. be terrified. do it anyway. you are on the precipice of changing your life. and you can't even imagine how good it's going to get when you find the courage to open your eyes.

you're not wrong for wanting love. for seeking community. for wishing for lifelong friendships. they say we are wired for connection. we are meant to hold and be held. our bodies were built for hugs and kisses. for belly laughs. for gathering and eating and singing and dancing. we were made to bring joy to each other. but society has separated us. turned us into means of production. for greed and for the gain of a small few. so be brave. admit you yearn. tell your people you want to hold them close, and do it. we only have so little time. open your heart so it can find other hearts like yours.

three of cups

hold hands with me
art isn't solitary
spirit is connectivity
flowing in community
see yourself in me
seventy percent water
reflective
together we are infinite
together we are the sea

on days you feel small
on days you feel weak
like you'll never amount
to anything at all
remember that you're a reflection
of all the love you've ever felt
and all the love you've ever given

just a reminder that you don't know what's going to happen tomorrow. you could meet someone new, a best friend, a lover or just someone who makes you laugh. you could make someone's day. get a message that changes your life. or meet someone who helps you learn how to love yourself a little more. you could get a sign from the universe that you're actually doing exactly what you're supposed to be doing. tomorrow could be the best day you've had in a while. and sometimes all it takes is one more day.

the kids on my street have a trampoline
and they use it
the kids on my street play road hockey
and get out of the way when cars come
they put on art shows
make homemade dog treats
computers didn't ruin anything
we're all still here
breathing
the kids are getting oxygen

what if your sole purpose in life isn't to find a soulmate
what if it's to excavate every little part of your soul
but not in a love yourself way
in an unlimited curiosity kind of way
what if you're meant to leave judgment at the door
and just discover every last drop of you
just as you are

*i can't
lose love
because it's
always
within me*

for the dreamers

you can see through the looking glass, but not everyone has your vision. not everyone understands that life is full of portals. that you can turn what you imagine into something you can touch. now is the time to shake hands with your future self, to have blind faith that the life that's been swirling around in your head is so close to being yours. i know you're scared. i know it's hard to be sure when so few people can see what you see. i know transformation feels like a heavy leather coat when you'd prefer a light jacket. but the weight of it all will be worth it. i promise.

everything is beautiful
and alive
and so am i

i'm really proud of my messy little life. that it's hard but i'm still trying. that it's not perfect but it's not supposed to be. i'm proud of the figuring things out, of the ups and downs. that i give myself space to make mistakes and learn from them. part of what's beautiful about me is that i'm flawed. i don't always know what to do. i get confused. i get sad, my emotions aren't logical. my thoughts aren't often rooted in reality. but i'm learning to see through them. and i'm learning to put down the façade. because tricking people into thinking i'm perfect was exhausting. and i just want to be all of me, the good parts and the parts i've been told to hide.

i wanna give new life to old things
i want worn-in leather
wedding bands
from lovers who have passed on
jugs and jars with knicks and memories
art that made someone smile for years
marble ashtrays will now
store my things
a wooden jewelry box
i'll fix the springs
history is beautiful
objects store memory
all i want is to find the gem
make something old feel new again

please look into the mirror

when i look at my body
i see Aphrodite
sorry your billions
spent to breed my self resent
went to waste

i spent most of my life trying to avoid being a reflection of someone else because i was afraid of being seen. but the more reflections we have, the more light we create. and if we all see each other's darkness, welcome it with warmth, hold its hand, the darkness becomes a little less scary. a little easier to carry. so i'll absorb your dark and reflect your light. and when i look at you, and you look at me, there will be rainbows in our eyes. and when i hold your hand, and you hold mine, we'll remember that we were never alone in the first place.

please look into the mirror

i am not a machine
i want to breathe life into things

when i look back at some of the biggest decisions i've made in my life, the scariest changes, i see myself as a totally different person. but i think that's because in hindsight, i mainly see the bravery. i forget about the shaky hands, the anxiety, the uncertainty. and sometimes i need to remind myself that the only reason i've ever been able to be courageous is because i pushed through the fear. i've never made a big life decision without being terrified. but maybe the fact that i look back at past me and see the bravery is the reminder i need that i still have it in me. and that when i look back on today, i won't remember my shaky hands. i'll just be proud of myself for having the courage to take the leap.

"how are you?"

i've been taking medication / feeling less scattered / having salt baths / singing at the top of my lungs / remembering why i write / remembering what hope feels like / doing things in a more logical order / making campfires / listening to records / obsessing over the color brown / painting my own nails / breathing / thinking about the sea / thinking before i respond / watching my nephew grow up / remembering what hope feels like / watching myself grow up / what am i if not hope persisting?

maybe i don't need to think about money
or bills
maybe i just need to sit in the grass
listen to the birds
wind blowing through the trees
get a coffee somewhere local
a croissant
give some to my dog
pat her head
maybe i need to be more afraid of dying
and less afraid of living

bringer of joy

i first met beatrice in july of 2018, four months after my first book came out. i did not become an overnight success and because of the immense pressure i put on myself and the book, i needed immediate rescuing.

enter beatrice. i found her in an online ad—her owner was moving? or getting divorced? or getting a new job? or all three? (still unclear) and she was the first french bulldog puppy i had seen with a longer snout (easier breathing felt more ethical to me). her name was originally peach. she peed on her previous owner's carpet a few minutes after i greeted her. definitely not because she was excited about meeting me–it more felt like an act of protest. but then i held her in my arms. and just like that, she was my dog.

why beatrice? when i was in high school, one of my favorite twitter comedians named their daughter bea and i hadn't been able to get it out of my head since. it was absolutely going to be the name of my first child. or dog.

having a puppy while depressed was extremely challenging. she pooed in her crate after being inside my house for only two minutes. she ate rocks, cigarette butts, and will still eat almost anything she can fit into her mouth.

but she also took me on walks every day. and i started paying attention to flowers because she sniffed them all. and i spent less time on my phone. and i noticed the wind, and leaves falling, and seasons changing in a way i never had before. because i saw it all through her eyes, too.

a few months after getting bea, i looked up the meaning of her name. it means 'bringer of joy.' and in the darkest part of my life up until that point, joy was exactly what she brought me.

i heard somewhere that your subconscious can't differentiate between what you say about someone else and what you say about yourself. so any words you say about others—whether loving or nasty—your subconscious interprets them as something you're saying about yourself.

because i have beatrice in my life, there are so many more loving words shared. and when i say she's the cutest girl in the world, maybe a part of my subconscious thinks i'm saying it about me. or when i say i love her with my whole heart, maybe inner me thinks i mean that about me too. and when i say i'm so grateful to be alive at the same time as her, i hope a part of me hears that i feel lucky to experience my soul in this body.

bea was my first mirror of unconditional love, and she brings joy to spaces that previously only knew darkness.

dogs can't read (as far as i know) but regardless–

i love you, bea

acknowledgements

this year was really hard for me. i felt burnt out, uninspired, a little like a hasbeen. i wouldn't have gotten through it all and wouldn't have written this book if it wasn't for:

you, dear reader! thank you for supporting me through six poetry collections. for stacking them on your shelves and nightstands, for returning to them when you need solace, to feel understood, to cry. this year i really remembered that you are my ultimate reflection and when i write for me, i'm writing for you, too.

jess, i love you and our love and that you support my dreams and my eccentricities and my need to be a tortured lone artist some of the time.

lacey, thank you for bringing three of cups energy into my life and sharing your spirit, you really helped me make it to the finish line.

mckenzie, thank you for inspiring me with your art and being a cocreator.

to my family and friends, thank you for buying all my books, for showcasing them in your homes, for being the first to write reviews, and my number one fans. this career can be lonely but i'm not lonely in life because of you.

about the author

michaela angemeer (she/they) is a queer canadian poet who's passionate about sharing her healing journey and inspiring readers to spend more time with their feelings.

they've published five best-selling collections of poetry including *when he leaves you, you'll come back to yourself, please love me at my worst, poems for the signs,* and *there is room for all of you here.*

michaela's newest book, *please look into the mirror,* is about facing the darkness to find light. separated into three sections: glass, mirror, and reflection, it's about the mother wound, gaining a deeper sense of self, learning to take accountability and finding relief in cycle breaking.

michaela lives in kitchener, ontario with her frenchton, bea. you can find her intently browsing thrift stores, ordering tapas at local restaurants or on her couch yapping to her girlfriend.

get in touch on tiktok & instagram: @michaelapoetry
get the rest of their books: michaelapoetry.com

get the whole collection

you'll come back to yourself
explores themes of lost love, infidelity, depression, body image, and ultimately the power people have in learning to choose themselves. separated into three sections: holding on, ouroboros, and letting go, this collection is a cyclical exploration of self-discovery.

please love me at my worst
a collection of four sections of poetry inspired by loneliness, unrequited love, and not being able to let go of past relationships. written during the 2020 quarantine, the book is a reflection of what it means to yearn for people who are unavailable and how important it is to focus on self-love and healing.

poems for the signs

starting with aries and ending with pisces, it's a collection about looking for love, self-reflection, depression, healing ancestral patterns, and finding beauty in being alone. it has themes of finding yourself, dating, family, grief and loss.

there is room for all of you here

this collection is an excavation of the past that leads to a celebration of queer love. separated into three sections: stumbling, falling, and landing, it's about complicated family relationships, reconciling with your anxious attachment style, finding a healthy love, and building something you hope will last.

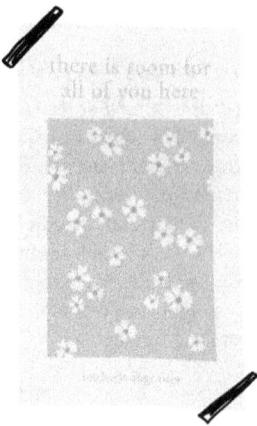

www.ingramcontent.com/pod-product-compliance
Lightning Source LLC
LaVergne TN
LVHW041545070426
835507LV00011B/931